I0710742

This Book Belongs to

....

....

....

MERRY CHRISTMAS

Color Test

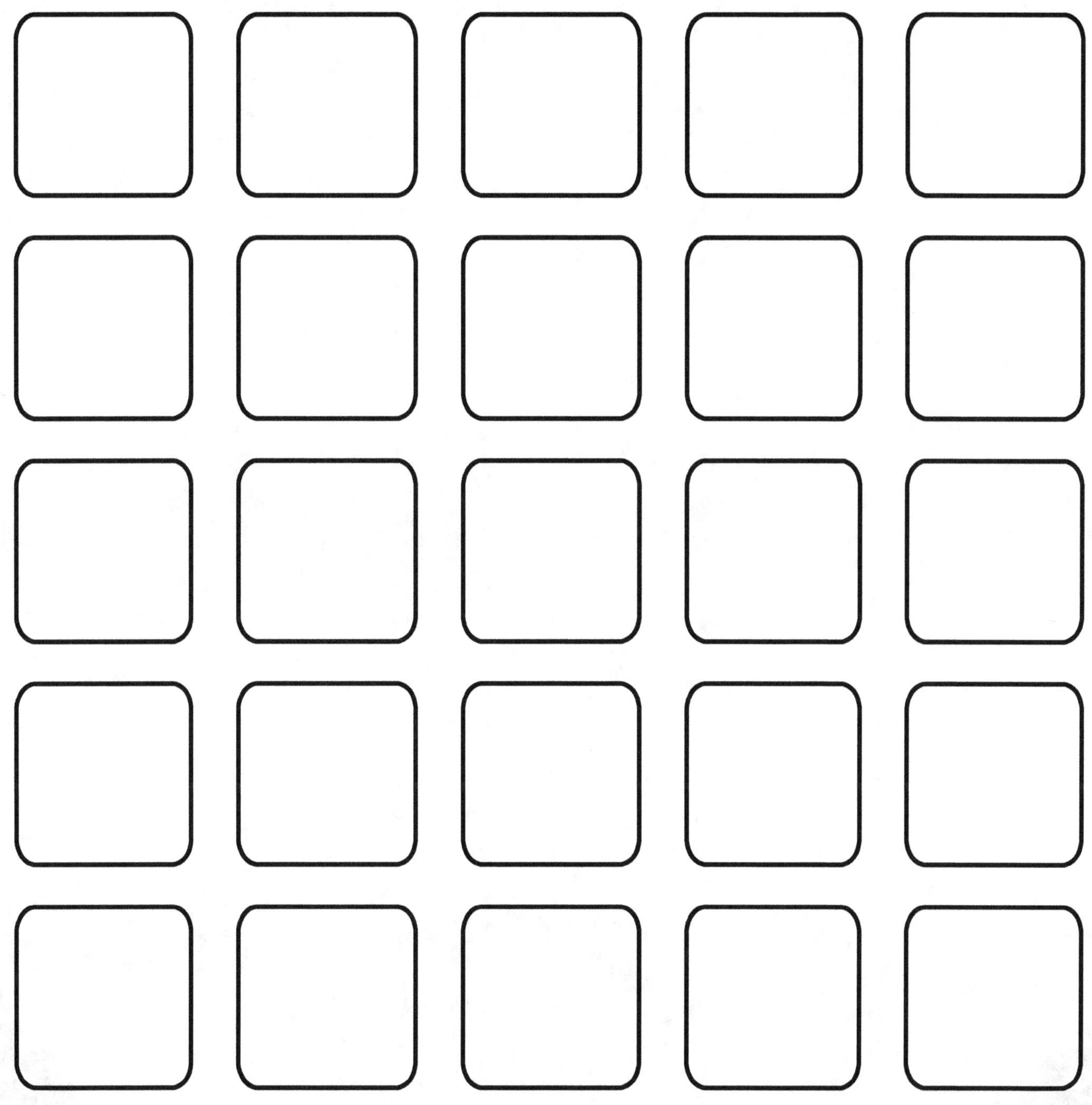

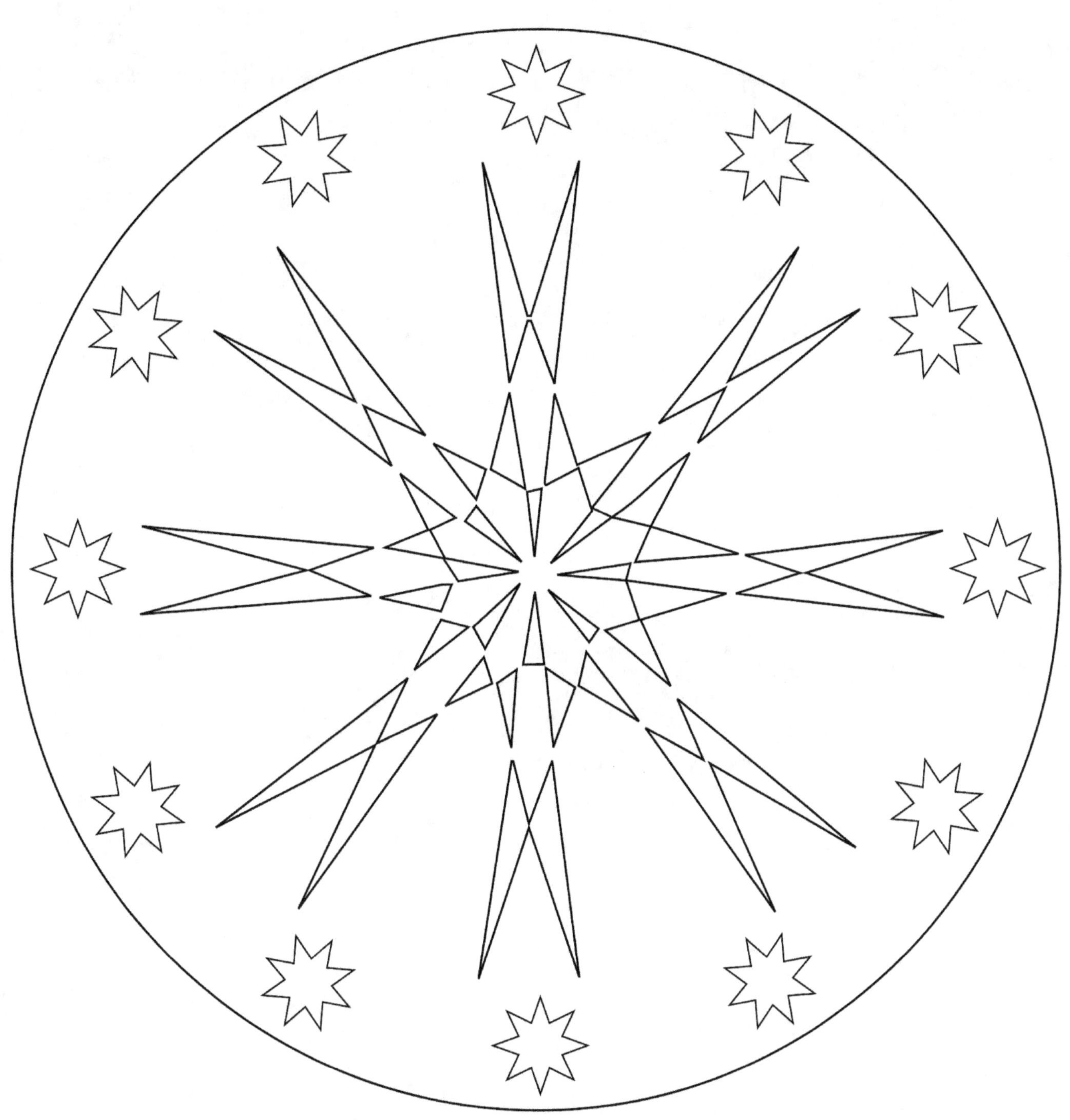

Merry
Christmas

Merry Christmas

JESUS

Merry
Christmas

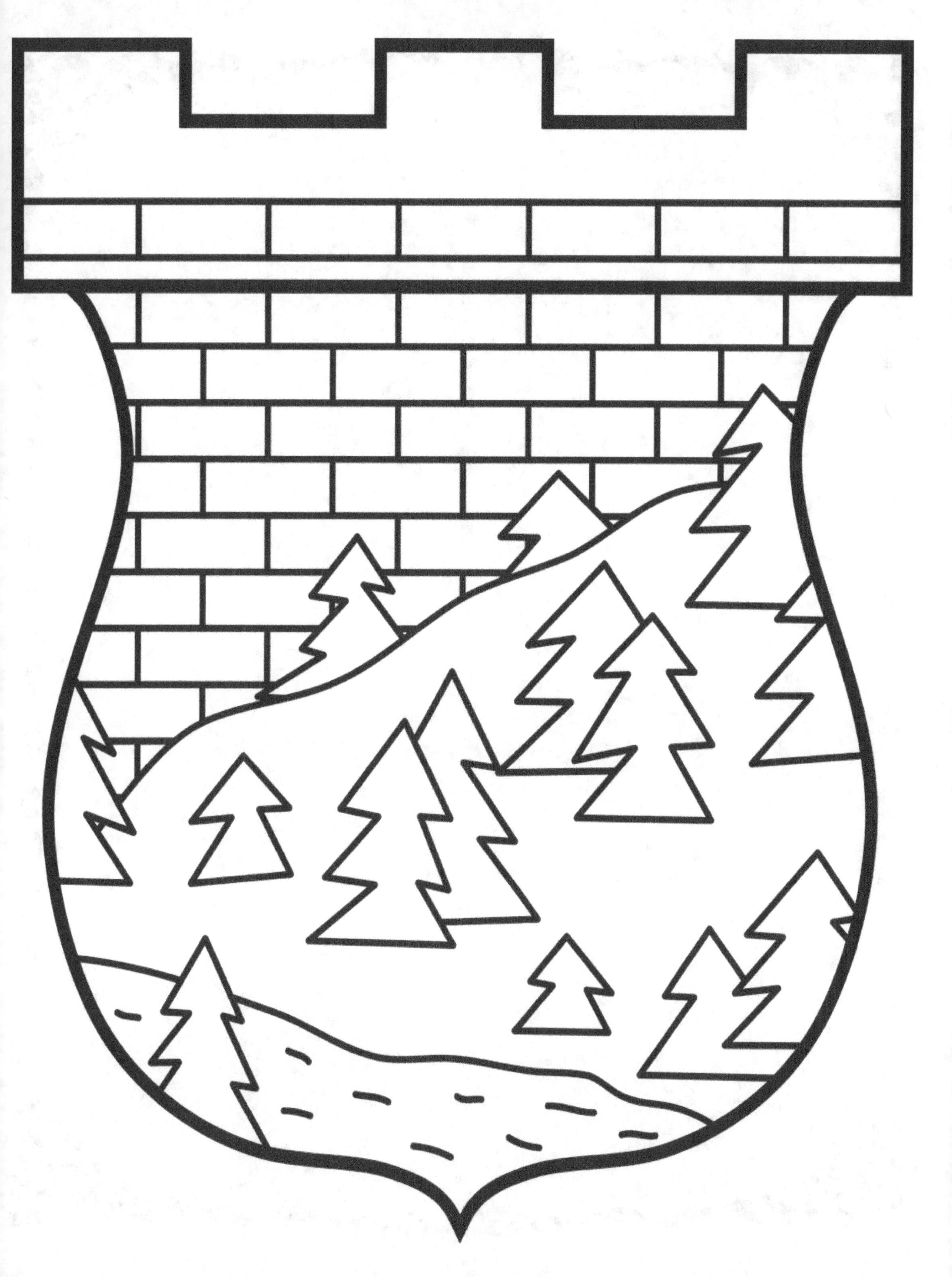

www.ingramcontent.com/pod-product-compliance
Lightning Source LLC
Chambersburg PA
CBHW081444250726
48662CB00009B/2938